CW00894809

THE BIG BOOK OF
STANDARDS

PIANO VOCAL GUITAR

THE BIG BOOK OF
STANDARDS

HAL LEONARD EUROPE

Distributed by Music Sales

Published by
Hal Leonard Europe
A Music Sales / Hal Leonard Joint Venture Company
14-15 Berners Street, London W1T 3LJ, UK.

Exclusive Distributors:
Music Sales Limited
Distribution Centre, Newmarket Road,
Bury St Edmunds, Suffolk IP33 3YB, UK.

Order No. HLE90004002
ISBN: 978-1-84938-634-0

This book © Copyright 2011 Hal Leonard Europe
Unauthorised reproduction of any part of this
publication by any means including photocopying
is an infringement of copyright.

Printed in the USA.

www.musicsales.com

ALL THE THINGS YOU ARE

from VERY WARM FOR MAY

Lyrics by OSCAR HAMMERSTEIN II
Music by JEROME KERN

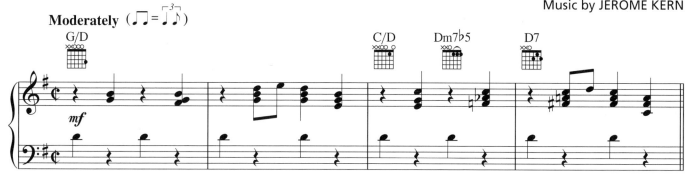

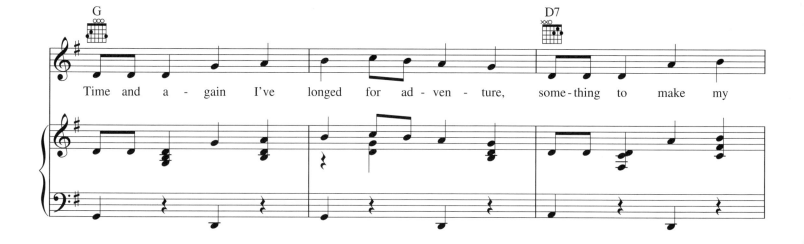

Time and a-gain I've longed for ad-ven-ture, some-thing to make my

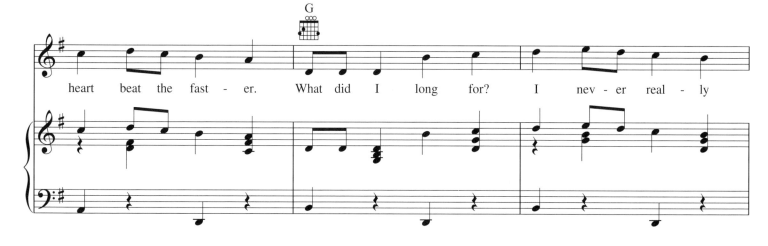

heart beat the fast-er. What did I long for? I nev-er real-ly

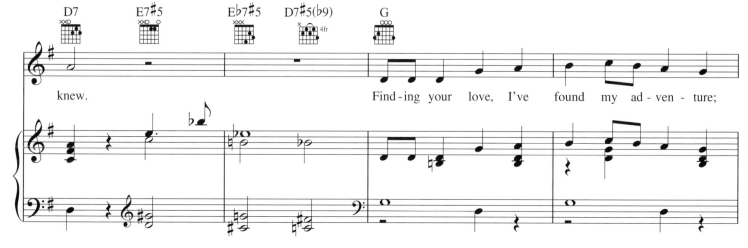

knew. Find-ing your love, I've found my ad-ven-ture;

Copyright © 1939 UNIVERSAL - POLYGRAM INTERNATIONAL PUBLISHING, INC.
Copyright Renewed
All Rights Reserved   Used by Permission

APRIL IN PARIS

Words by E.Y. "YIP" HARBURG
Music by VERNON DUKE

Copyright © 1932 by Kay Duke Music and Glocca Morra Music
Copyright Renewed
All Rights for Kay Duke Music Administered by Universal Music - MGB Songs
All Rights for Glocca Morra Music Administered by Next Decade Entertainment, Inc.
International Copyright Secured   All Rights Reserved

BETWEEN THE DEVIL AND THE DEEP BLUE SEA

from RHYTHMANIA

Lyric by TED KOEHLER
Music by HAROLD ARLEN

(last time) Is there an-y-one a-round who can-not see it's the well-known run-a-round you're giv-ing me?

Copyright © 1931 (Renewed 1958) FRED AHLERT MUSIC GROUP, TED KOEHLER MUSIC CO. and S.A. MUSIC CO.
All Rights for FRED AHLERT MUSIC GROUP and TED KOEHLER MUSIC CO. Administered by BUG MUSIC
All Rights Reserved   Used by Permission

BEYOND THE BLUE HORIZON
from the Paramount Picture MONTE CARLO

Words by LEO ROBIN
Music by RICHARD A. WHITING
and W. FRANKE HARLING

Copyright © 1930 (Renewed 1957) by Famous Music LLC
International Copyright Secured   All Rights Reserved

gone all my grief and woe. What

mat - ter where I go if I am free? _____

Moderately (In 2)

N.C.

Be -

Moderately fast

yond the blue ho - ri - zon

24

BLUESETTE

Words by NORMAN GIMBEL
Music by JEAN THIELEMANS

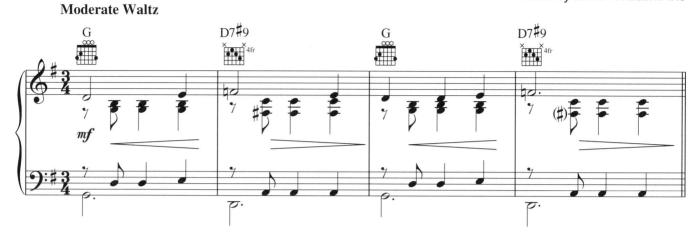

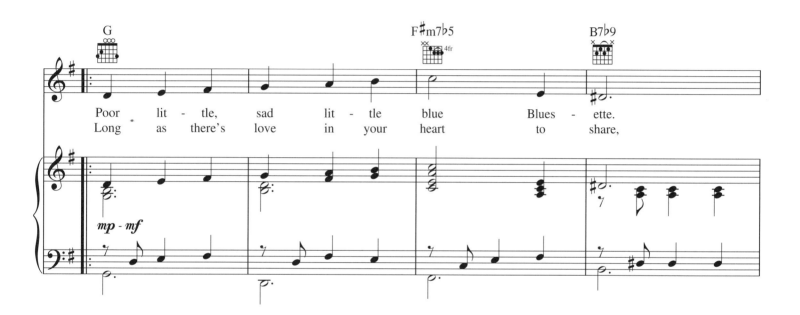

Poor lit - tle, sad lit - tle blue Blues - ette.
Long as there's sad love in your blue heart Blues to share,

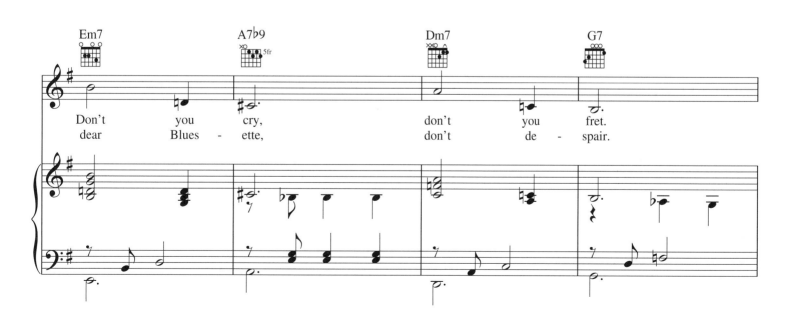

Don't you cry, don't you fret.
dear Blues - ette, don't de - spair.

Copyright © 1963, 1964 SONGS OF UNIVERSAL, INC.
Copyright Renewed; Words Renewed 1992 by NORMAN GIMBEL for the World and
Assigned to NEW THUNDER MUSIC, INC. Administered by GIMBEL MUSIC GROUP, INC.
(P.O. Box 15221, Beverly Hills, CA 90209 USA)
All Rights Reserved   Used by Permission

CALL ME IRRESPONSIBLE
from the Paramount Picture PAPA'S DELICATE CONDITION

Words by SAMMY CAHN
Music by JAMES VAN HEUSEN

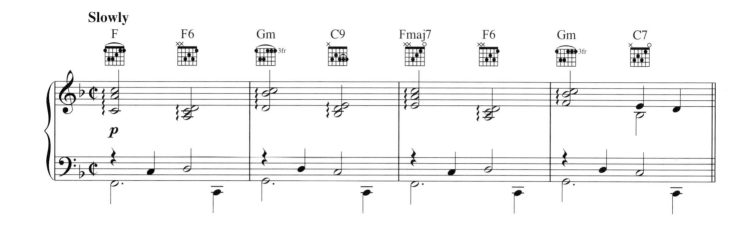

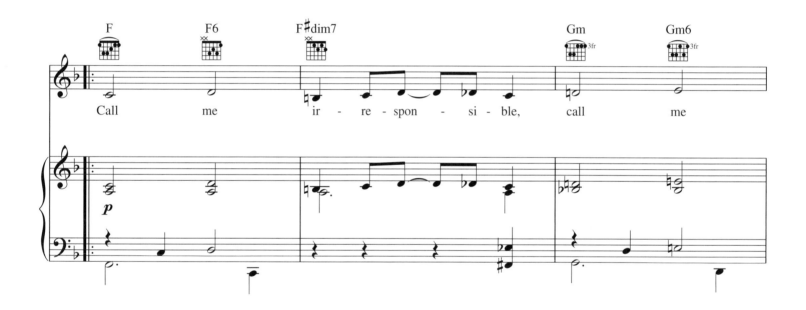

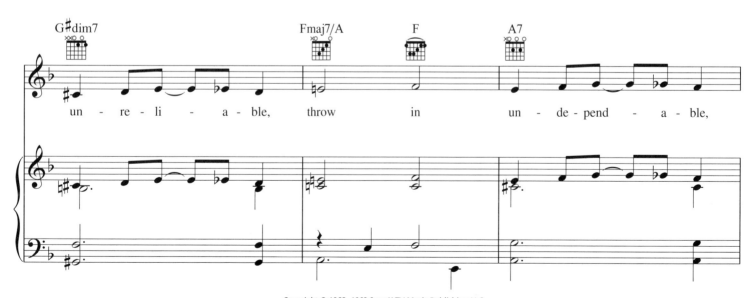

Copyright © 1962, 1963 Sony/ATV Music Publishing LLC
Copyright Renewed
All Rights Administered by Sony/ATV Music Publishing LLC, 8 Music Square West, Nashville, TN 37203
International Copyright Secured   All Rights Reserved

too. _____ Do my

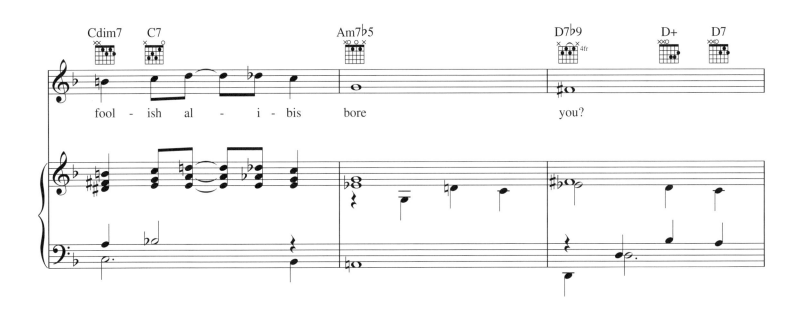

fool - ish al - i - bis bore you?

Well, I'm not too clev - er. I just a -

CAN'T HELP LOVIN' DAT MAN

from SHOW BOAT

Lyrics by OSCAR HAMMERSTEIN II
Music by JEROME KERN

Slowly

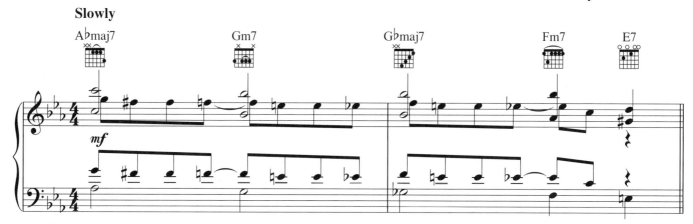

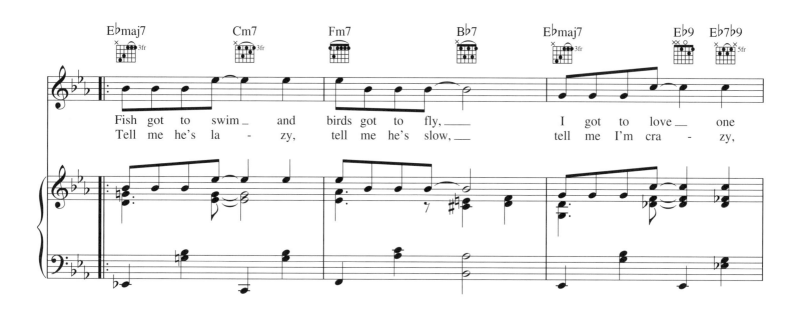

Fish got to swim __ and birds got to fly, ___ I got to love __ one
Tell me he's la - zy, tell me he's slow, ___ tell me I'm cra - zy,

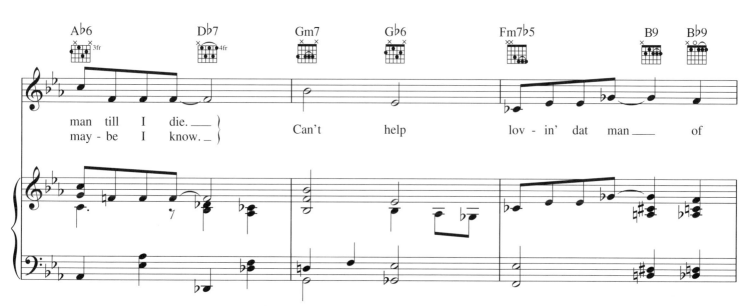

man till I die. __ } Can't help lov - in' dat man ___ of
may - be I know. __ }

Copyright © 1927 UNIVERSAL - POLYGRAM INTERNATIONAL PUBLISHING, INC.
Copyright Renewed
All Rights Reserved   Used by Permission

CARAVAN

Words and Music by DUKE ELLINGTON,
IRVING MILLS and JUAN TIZOL

Copyright © 1937 Sony/ATV Music Publishing LLC and EMI Mills Music Inc. in the U.S.A.
Copyright Renewed
All Rights on behalf of Sony/ATV Music Publishing LLC Administered by Sony/ATV Music Publishing LLC, 8 Music Square West, Nashville, TN 37203
Rights for the world outside the U.S.A. Administered by EMI Mills Music Inc. (Publishing) and Alfred Publishing Co., Inc. (Print)
International Copyright Secured   All Rights Reserved

COCKTAILS FOR TWO

from the Paramount Picture MURDER AT THE VANITIES

Words and Music by ARTHUR JOHNSTON
and SAM COSLOW

Copyright © 1934 (Renewed 1961) by Famous Music Corporation
International Copyright Secured   All Rights Reserved

48

DARN THAT DREAM

Lyric by EDDIE DE LANGE
Music by JIMMY VAN HEUSEN

Darn that dream I
Darn your lips and

dream each night, you say you love me and you
darn your eyes, they say lift me high a - bove the

hold me tight, but when I a - wake you're
moon lit skies, then I tum - ble out of

Copyright © 1939 WB Music Corp.
Copyright Renewed, Assigned and Copyright © 1968 by Scarsdale Music Corporation and Music Sales Corporation
International Copyright Secured   All Rights Reserved
Used by Permission

50

DEARLY BELOVED

from YOU WERE NEVER LOVELIER

Music by JEROME KERN
Words by JOHNNY MERCER

Poco allegretto

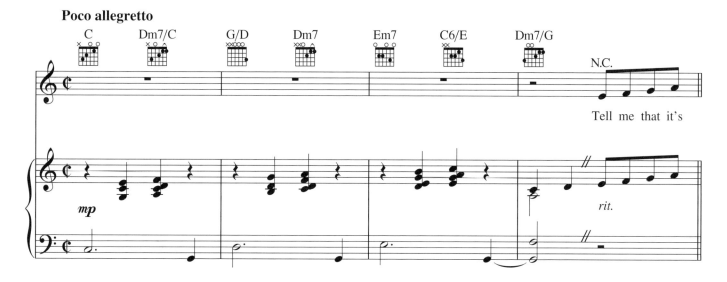

Tell me that it's

true, _____ tell me you a - gree, _____ I was meant for

you, _____ you were meant for me. _____

Copyright © 1942 UNIVERSAL - POLYGRAM INTERNATIONAL PUBLISHING, INC.
Copyright Renewed
All Rights Reserved   Used by Permission

DO NOTHIN' TILL
YOU HEAR FROM ME

Words and Music by DUKE ELLINGTON
and BOB RUSSELL

Copyright © 1943 Sony/ATV Music Publishing LLC and Music Sales Corporation
Copyright Renewed
All Rights on behalf of Sony/ATV Music Publishing LLC Administered by Sony/ATV Music Publishing LLC, 8 Music Square West, Nashville, TN 37203
International Copyright Secured   All Rights Reserved

DON'T GET AROUND MUCH ANYMORE

from SOPHISTICATED LADY

Words and Music by DUKE ELLINGTON
and BOB RUSSELL

Copyright © 1942 Sony/ATV Music Publishing LLC and Music Sales Corporation
Copyright Renewed
All Rights on behalf of Sony/ATV Music Publishing LLC Administered by Sony/ATV Music Publishing LLC, 8 Music Square West, Nashville, TN 37203
International Copyright Secured   All Rights Reserved

60

EASY LIVING
Theme from the Paramount Picture EASY LIVING

Words and Music by LEO ROBIN
and RALPH RAINGER

Copyright © 1937 Sony/ATV Music Publishing LLC
Copyright Renewed
All Rights Administered by Sony/ATV Music Publishing LLC, 8 Music Square West, Nashville, TN 37203
International Copyright Secured   All Rights Reserved

A FINE ROMANCE

from SWING TIME

Words by DOROTHY FIELDS
Music by JEROME KERN

Copyright © 1936 UNIVERSAL - POLYGRAM INTERNATIONAL PUBLISHING, INC. and ALDI MUSIC
Copyright Renewed
Print Rights for ALDI MUSIC in the U.S. Controlled and Administered by HAPPY ASPEN MUSIC LLC c/o SHAPIRO, BERNSTEIN & CO., INC.
All Rights Reserved   Used by Permission

68

FLY ME TO THE MOON
(In Other Words)
featured in the Motion Picture ONCE AROUND

Words and Music by
BART HOWARD

TRO - © Copyright 1954 (Renewed) Hampshire House Publishing Corp., New York, NY
International Copyright Secured
All Rights Reserved Including Public Performance For Profit
Used by Permission

HERE'S THAT RAINY DAY

from CARNIVAL IN FLANDERS

Words by JOHNNY BURKE
Music by JIMMY VAN HEUSEN

Copyright © 1949 by Bourne Co. (ASCAP) and Dorsey Bros. Music, a division of Music Sales Corporation (ASCAP)
Copyright Renewed
International Copyright Secured   All Rights Reserved
Reprinted by Permission

GEORGIA ON MY MIND

Words by STUART GORRELL
Music by HOAGY CARMICHAEL

Copyright © 1930 by Peermusic III, Ltd.
Copyright Renewed
International Copyright Secured   All Rights Reserved

I DON'T WANT TO WALK WITHOUT YOU

from the Paramount Picture SWEATER GIRL

Words by FRANK LOESSER
Music by JULE STYNE

Copyright © 1941 Sony/ATV Music Publishing LLC
Copyright Renewed
All Rights Administered by Sony/ATV Music Publishing LLC, 8 Music Square West, Nashville, TN 37203
International Copyright Secured   All Rights Reserved

83

I HEAR MUSIC

from the Paramount Picture DANCING ON A DIME

Words by FRANK LOESSER
Music by BURTON LANE

Copyright © 1940 Sony/ATV Music Publishing LLC
Copyright Renewed
All Rights Administered by Sony/ATV Music Publishing LLC, 8 Music Square West, Nashville, TN 37203
International Copyright Secured   All Rights Reserved

I LEFT MY HEART IN SAN FRANCISCO

Words by DOUGLASS CROSS
Music by GEORGE CORY

© 1954 (Renewed 1982) COLGEMS-EMI MUSIC INC.
All Rights Reserved   International Copyright Secured   Used by Permission

I WISH I DIDN'T LOVE YOU SO

from the Paramount Picture THE PERILS OF PAULINE

Words and Music by
FRANK LOESSER

Copyright © 1947 Sony/ATV Music Publishing LLC
Copyright Renewed
All Rights Administered by Sony/ATV Music Publishing LLC, 8 Music Square West, Nashville, TN 37203
International Copyright Secured   All Rights Reserved

I REMEMBER YOU

from the Paramount Picture THE FLEET'S IN

Words by JOHNNY MERCER
Music by VICTOR SCHERTZINGER

Copyright © 1942 Sony/ATV Music Publishing LLC
Copyright Renewed
All Rights Administered by Sony/ATV Music Publishing LLC, 8 Music Square West, Nashville, TN 37203
International Copyright Secured   All Rights Reserved

I'LL NEVER SMILE AGAIN

Words and Music by
RUTH LOWE

Copyright © 1939 UNIVERSAL MUSIC CORP.
Copyright Renewed
All Rights Reserved   Used by Permission

I'M BEGINNING TO SEE THE LIGHT

Words and Music by DON GEORGE, JOHNNY HODGES,
DUKE ELLINGTON and HARRY JAMES

Copyright © 1944 Sony/ATV Music Publishing LLC, Chappell & Co. and Ricki Music Company in the U.S.A.
Copyright Renewed
All Rights on behalf of Sony/ATV Music Publishing LLC Administered by Sony/ATV Music Publishing LLC, 8 Music Square West, Nashville, TN 37203
All Rights on behalf of Ricki Music Company Administered by WB Music Corp.
Rights for the world outside the U.S.A. Administered by Chappell & Co.
International Copyright Secured   All Rights Reserved

I'LL REMEMBER APRIL

Words and Music by PAT JOHNSTON,
DON RAYE and GENE DE PAUL

© 1941, 1942 (Renewed) PIC CORPORATION and UNIVERSAL MUSIC CORP.
All Rights Reserved

I'VE GOT THE WORLD ON A STRING

Lyric by TED KOEHLER
Music by HAROLD ARLEN

Mer - ry month of May, sun - ny

© 1932 (Renewed 1960) TED KOEHLER MUSIC CO. (ASCAP)/Administered by BUG MUSIC and S.A. MUSIC CO.
All Rights Reserved   Used by Permission

skies of blue, clouds have rolled a - way and the sun peeps thru, may ex -

press _____ hap - pi - ness. _____

___ Joy you may de - fine in a thou - sand ways, but a

case like mine needs a "spe - cial phrase" to re - veal _____

IN A SENTIMENTAL MOOD

Words and Music by DUKE ELLINGTON,
IRVING MILLS and MANNY KURTZ

Copyright © 1935 Sony/ATV Music Publishing LLC and EMI Mills Music Inc. in the U.S.A.
Copyright Renewed
All Rights on behalf of Sony/ATV Music Publishing LLC Administered by Sony/ATV Music Publishing LLC, 8 Music Square West, Nashville, TN 37203
Rights for the world outside the U.S.A. Administered by EMI Mills Music Inc. (Publishing) and Alfred Publishing Co., Inc. (Print)
International Copyright Secured   All Rights Reserved

IN THE COOL, COOL, COOL OF THE EVENING

from the Paramount Picture HERE COMES THE GROOM

Words by JOHNNY MERCER
Music by HOAGY CARMICHAEL

Copyright © 1951 Sony/ATV Music Publishing LLC
Copyright Renewed
All Rights Administered by Sony/ATV Music Publishing LLC, 8 Music Square West, Nashville, TN 37203
International Copyright Secured   All Rights Reserved

ISN'T IT ROMANTIC?

from the Paramount Picture LOVE ME TONIGHT

Words by LORENZ HART
Music by RICHARD RODGERS

Copyright © 1932 Sony/ATV Music Publishing LLC
Copyright Renewed
All Rights Administered by Sony/ATV Music Publishing LLC, 8 Music Square West, Nashville, TN 37203
International Copyright Secured   All Rights Reserved

IT COULD HAPPEN TO YOU

from the Paramount Picture AND THE ANGELS SING

Words by JOHNNY BURKE
Music by JAMES VAN HEUSEN

Copyright © 1944 Sony/ATV Music Publishing LLC
Copyright Renewed
All Rights Administered by Sony/ATV Music Publishing LLC, 8 Music Square West, Nashville, TN 37203
International Copyright Secured   All Rights Reserved

IT'S EASY TO REMEMBER

from the Paramount Picture MISSISSIPPI

Words by LORENZ HART
Music by RICHARD RODGERS

Copyright © 1934 Sony/ATV Music Publishing LLC
Copyright Renewed
All Rights Administered by Sony/ATV Music Publishing LLC, 8 Music Square West, Nashville, TN 37203
International Copyright Secured   All Rights Reserved

JUNE IN JANUARY
from the Paramount Picture HERE IS MY HEART

Words and Music by LEO ROBIN
and RALPH RAINGER

Copyright © 1934 Sony/ATV Music Publishing LLC
Copyright Renewed
All Rights Administered by Sony/ATV Music Publishing LLC, 8 Music Square West, Nashville, TN 37203
International Copyright Secured   All Rights Reserved

IT'S IMPOSSIBLE
(Somos Novios)

English Lyric by SID WAYNE
Spanish Words and Music by
ARMANDO MANZANERO

Copyright © 1968 by Universal Music Publishing MGB Edim., S.A. de C.V.
Copyright Renewed
All Rights for the U.S. Administered by Universal Music - MGB Songs
International Copyright Secured   All Rights Reserved

JUST AS MUCH AS EVER

Words and Music by CHARLES SINGLETON
and LARRY COLEMAN

© 1957 (Renewed 1985) SCREEN GEMS-EMI MUSIC INC.
All Rights Reserved   International Copyright Secured   Used by Permission

LOLLIPOPS AND ROSES

Words and Music by
TONY VELONA

Copyright © 1960, 1962 UNIVERSAL MUSIC CORP.
Copyright Renewed
All Rights Reserved   Used by Permission

THE LADY'S IN LOVE WITH YOU

from the Paramount Picture SOME LIKE IT HOT

Words by FRANK LOESSER
Music by BURTON LANE

Copyright © 1939 (Renewed 1966) by Paramount Music Corporation
International Copyright Secured   All Rights Reserved

148

LOVE IS JUST AROUND THE CORNER

from the Paramount Picture HERE IS MY HEART

Words and Music by LEO ROBIN
and LEWIS E. GENSLER

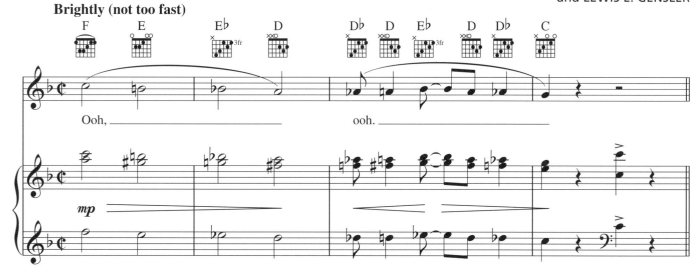

Brightly (not too fast)

Ooh, _____ ooh. _____

Beau - ti - ful mir - a - cle, par - don my lyr - i - cal rhap - so - dy, _____

_____ but can't you see _____ you've cap - tured me? _____

Copyright © 1934 Sony/ATV Music Publishing LLC
Copyright Renewed
All Rights Administered by Sony/ATV Music Publishing LLC, 8 Music Square West, Nashville, TN 37203
International Copyright Secured   All Rights Reserved

LOVE LETTERS
Theme from the Paramount Picture LOVE LETTERS

Words by EDWARD HEYMAN
Music by VICTOR YOUNG

Copyright © 1945 Sony/ATV Music Publishing LLC
Copyright Renewed
All Rights Administered by Sony/ATV Music Publishing LLC, 8 Music Square West, Nashville, TN 37203
International Copyright Secured   All Rights Reserved

156

LOVER
from the Paramount Picture LOVE ME TONIGHT

Words by LORENZ HART
Music by RICHARD RODGERS

Copyright © 1932 Sony/ATV Music Publishing LLC
Copyright Renewed
All Rights Administered by Sony/ATV Music Publishing LLC, 8 Music Square West, Nashville, TN 37203
International Copyright Secured   All Rights Reserved

MAKE BELIEVE

from SHOW BOAT

Lyrics by OSCAR HAMMERSTEIN II
Music by JEROME KERN

Copyright © 1927 UNIVERSAL - POLYGRAM INTERNATIONAL PUBLISHING, INC.
Copyright Renewed
All Rights Reserved   Used by Permission

LOVER, COME BACK TO ME

from THE NEW MOON

Lyrics by OSCAR HAMMERSTEIN II
Music by SIGMUND ROMBERG

Copyright © 1928 by Bambalina Music Publishing Co. and Warner Bros. Inc. in the United States
Copyright Renewed
All Rights on behalf of Bambalina Music Publishing Co. Administered by Williamson Music
International Copyright Secured   All Rights Reserved

MISTY

Words by JOHNNY BURKE
Music by ERROLL GARNER

Copyright © 1955 by Octave Music Publishing Corp., Marke Music Publishing Co., Inc., Reganesque Music, Limerick Music and My Dad's Songs, Inc.
Copyright Renewed 1982
All Rights for Marke Music Publishing Co., Inc. Administered by Universal Music - MGB Songs
All Rights for Reganesque Music, Limerick Music and My Dad's Songs, Inc. Administered by Spirit Two Music, Inc.
International Copyright Secured   All Rights Reserved

MONA LISA

from the Paramount Picture CAPTAIN CAREY, U.S.A.

Words and Music by JAY LIVINGSTON
and RAY EVANS

In a vil - la in a lit - tle old I - tal - ian town lives a girl whose beau - ty shames the rose. Man - y yearn to love her but their hopes all tum - ble down. What does she want? No one knows! Mo - na

Copyright © 1949 Sony/ATV Music Publishing LLC
Copyright Renewed
All Rights Administered by Sony/ATV Music Publishing LLC, 8 Music Square West, Nashville, TN 37203
International Copyright Secured   All Rights Reserved

MOON RIVER

from the Paramount Picture BREAKFAST AT TIFFANY'S

Words by JOHNNY MERCER
Music by HENRY MANCINI

Copyright © 1961 Sony/ATV Music Publishing LLC
Copyright Renewed
All Rights Administered by Sony/ATV Music Publishing LLC, 8 Music Square West, Nashville, TN 37203
International Copyright Secured   All Rights Reserved

MY IDEAL

from the Paramount Picture PLAYBOY OF PARIS

Words by LEO ROBIN
Music by RICHARD A. WHITING and NEWELL CHASE

Copyright © 1930 Sony/ATV Music Publishing LLC
Copyright Renewed
All Rights Administered by Sony/ATV Music Publishing LLC, 8 Music Square West, Nashville, TN 37203
International Copyright Secured   All Rights Reserved

MOONLIGHT BECOMES YOU
from the Paramount Picture ROAD TO MOROCCO

Words by JOHNNY BURKE
Music by JAMES VAN HEUSEN

Copyright © 1942 Sony/ATV Music Publishing LLC
Copyright Renewed
All Rights Administered by Sony/ATV Music Publishing LLC, 8 Music Square West, Nashville, TN 37203
International Copyright Secured   All Rights Reserved

MY OLD FLAME

from the Paramount Picture BELLE OF THE NINETIES

Words and Music by ARTHUR JOHNSTON
and SAM COSLOW

Copyright © 1934 Sony/ATV Music Publishing LLC
Copyright Renewed
All Rights Administered by Sony/ATV Music Publishing LLC, 8 Music Square West, Nashville, TN 37203
International Copyright Secured   All Rights Reserved

MY SILENT LOVE

Words by EDWARD HEYMAN
Music by DANA SUESSE

Moderately

You would on-ly spurn my love if I had shown it.

You would sure-ly turn my love a-way.

Copyright © 1932 Sony/ATV Music Publishing LLC
Copyright Renewed
All Rights Administered by Sony/ATV Music Publishing LLC, 8 Music Square West, Nashville, TN 37203
International Copyright Secured All Rights Reserved

THE NEARNESS OF YOU

from the Paramount Picture ROMANCE IN THE DARK

Words by NED WASHINGTON
Music by HOAGY CARMICHAEL

Copyright © 1937, 1940 Sony/ATV Music Publishing LLC
Copyright Renewed
All Rights Administered by Sony/ATV Music Publishing LLC, 8 Music Square West, Nashville, TN 37203
International Copyright Secured All Rights Reserved

OL' MAN RIVER

from SHOW BOAT

Lyrics by OSCAR HAMMERSTEIN II
Music by JEROME KERN

Copyright © 1927 UNIVERSAL - POLYGRAM INTERNATIONAL PUBLISHING, INC.
Copyright Renewed
All Rights Reserved   Used by Permission

204

ON A SLOW BOAT TO CHINA

By FRANK LOESSER

© 1948 (Renewed) FRANK MUSIC CORP.
All Rights Reserved

OUT OF NOWHERE

from the Paramount Picture DUDE RANCH

Words by EDWARD HEYMAN
Music by JOHNNY GREEN

Copyright © 1931 Sony/ATV Music Publishing LLC
Copyright Renewed
All Rights Administered by Sony/ATV Music Publishing LLC, 8 Music Square West, Nashville, TN 37203
International Copyright Secured   All Rights Reserved

PENTHOUSE SERENADE

Words and Music by WILL JASON
and VAL BURTON

Copyright © 1931 Sony/ATV Music Publishing LLC
Copyright Renewed; extended term of Copyright deriving from Val Burton and Will Jason assigned and effective July 13, 1987 to Range Road Music Inc. and Bug Music-Quartet Music
All Rights Administered in the U.S. by Range Road Music Inc.
All Rights outside the U.S. Administered by Sony/ATV Music Publishing LLC, 8 Music Square West, Nashville, TN 37203
International Copyright Secured   All Rights Reserved
Used by Permission

ROCKIN' CHAIR

Words and Music by
HOAGY CARMICHAEL

Copyright © 1929, 1930 by Songs Of Peer, Ltd.
Copyrights Renewed
International Copyright Secured   All Rights Reserved

PICK YOURSELF UP

from SWING TIME

Words by DOROTHY FIELDS
Music by JEROME KERN

Copyright © 1936 UNIVERSAL - POLYGRAM INTERNATIONAL PUBLISHING, INC. and ALDI MUSIC
Copyright Renewed
Print Rights for ALDI MUSIC in the U.S. Controlled and Administered by HAPPY ASPEN MUSIC LLC c/o SHAPIRO, BERNSTEIN & CO., INC.
All Rights Reserved   Used by Permission

228

SATIN DOLL
from SOPHISTICATED LADIES

Words by JOHNNY MERCER and BILLY STRAYHORN
Music by DUKE ELLINGTON

Copyright © 1958 Sony/ATV Music Publishing LLC, WB Music Corp. and Tempo Music, Inc. c/o Music Sales Corporation in the U.S.A.
Copyright Renewed
All Rights on behalf of Sony/ATV Music Publishing LLC Administered by Sony/ATV Music Publishing LLC, 8 Music Square West, Nashville, TN 37203
Rights for the world outside the U.S.A. Administered by Tempo Music, Inc. c/o Music Sales Corporation
International Copyright Secured   All Rights Reserved

232

SING, YOU SINNERS

from the Paramount Picture HONEY
Theme from the Paramount Picture SING, YOU SINNERS

Words and Music by SAM COSLOW
and W. FRANKE HARLING

Copyright © 1930 (Renewed 1957) by Famous Music Corporation
International Copyright Secured   All Rights Reserved

SKYLARK

Words by JOHNNY MERCER
Music by HOAGY CARMICHAEL

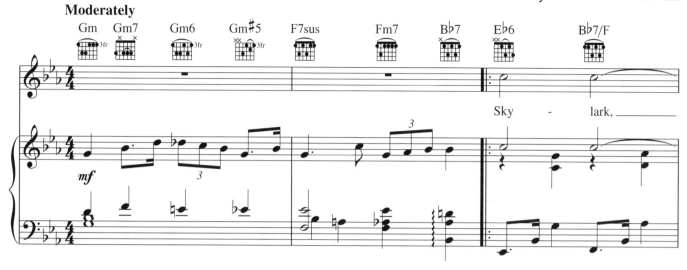

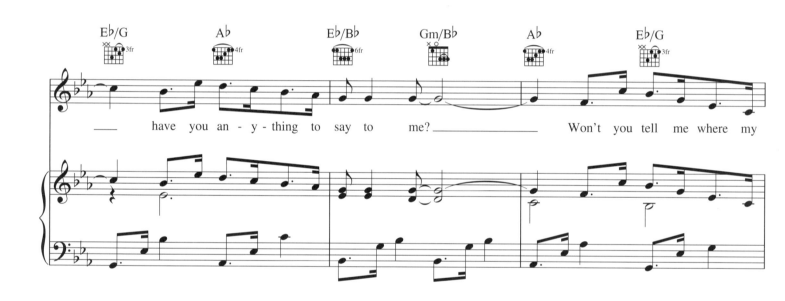

Copyright © 1941, 1942 by Songs Of Peer, Ltd. and WB Music Corp.
Copyright Renewed
International Copyright Secured   All Rights Reserved

SMALL FRY
from the Paramount Motion Picture SING, YOU SINNERS

Words by FRANK LOESSER
Music by HOAGY CARMICHAEL

Copyright © 1938 Sony/ATV Music Publishing LLC
Copyright Renewed
All Rights Administered by Sony/ATV Music Publishing LLC, 8 Music Square West, Nashville, TN 37213
International Copyright Secured   All Rights Reserved

SOMEBODY LOVES YOU

Words by CHARLIE TOBIAS
Music by PETER DE ROSE

© 1932 (Renewed) EDWIN H. MORRIS & COMPANY, A Division of MPL Music Publishing, Inc.
All Rights Reserved

SOPHISTICATED LADY

Words and Music by DUKE ELLINGTON,
IRVING MILLS and MITCHELL PARISH

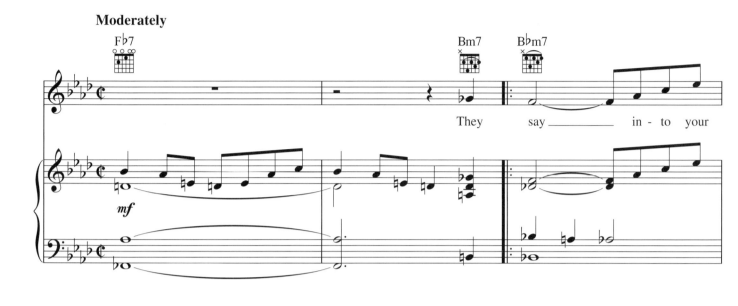

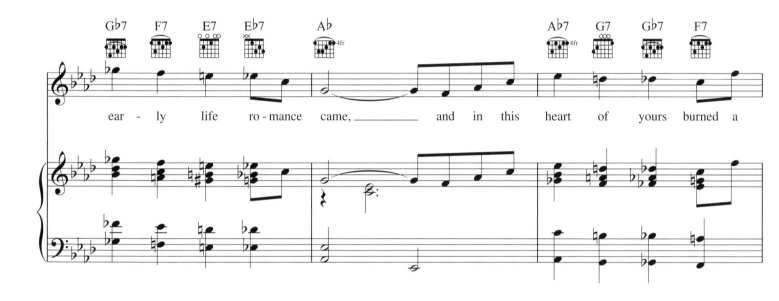

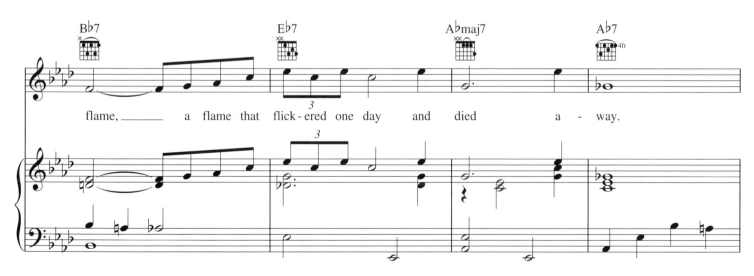

Copyright © 1933 Sony/ATV Music Publishing LLC and EMI Mills Music Inc. in the U.S.A.
Copyright Renewed
All Rights on behalf of Sony/ATV Music Publishing LLC Administered by Sony/ATV Music Publishing LLC, 8 Music Square West, Nashville, TN 37203
Rights for the world outside the U.S.A. Controlled by EMI Mills Music Inc. (Publishing) and Alfred Publishing Co., Inc. (Print)
International Copyright Secured   All Rights Reserved

STARDUST

Words by MITCHELL PARISH
Music by HOAGY CARMICHAEL

Copyright © 1928, 1929 by Songs Of Peer, Ltd. and EMI Mills Music, Inc.
Copyrights Renewed
All Rights outside the USA Controlled by EMI Mills Music, Inc. (Publishing) and Alfred Publishing Co., Inc. (Print)
International Copyright Secured   All Rights Reserved

SPEAK SOFTLY, LOVE
(Love Theme)
from the Paramount Picture THE GODFATHER

Words by LARRY KUSIK
Music by NINO ROTA

Copyright © 1972 Sony/ATV Music Publishing LLC
Copyright Renewed
All Rights Administered by Sony/ATV Music Publishing LLC, 8 Music Square West, Nashville, TN 37203
International Copyright Secured   All Rights Reserved

STELLA BY STARLIGHT

from the Paramount Picture THE UNINVITED

Words by NED WASHINGTON
Music by VICTOR YOUNG

Copyright © 1946 (Renewed 1973, 1974) by Famous Music LLC
International Copyright Secured   All Rights Reserved

THE SURREY WITH THE FRINGE ON TOP

from OKLAHOMA!

Lyrics by OSCAR HAMMERSTEIN II
Music by RICHARD RODGERS

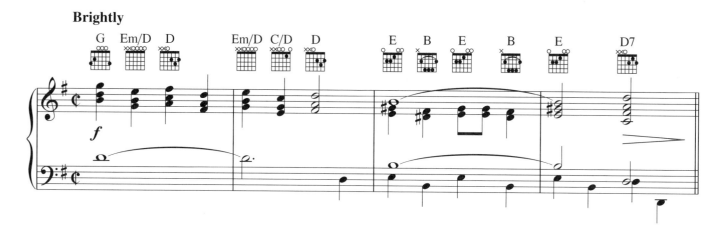

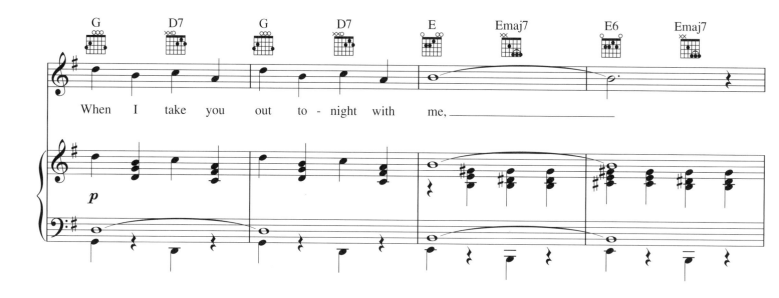

When I take you out to-night with me,

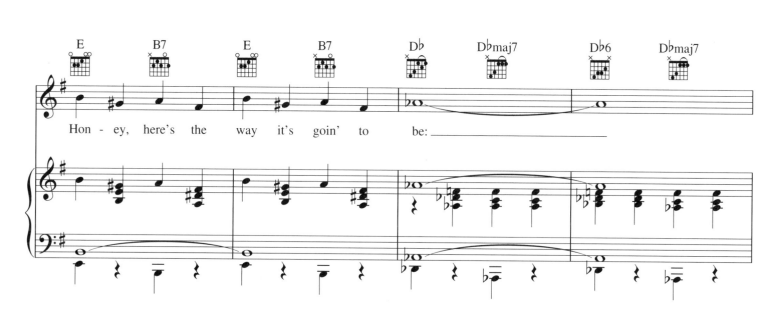

Hon-ey, here's the way it's goin' to be:

Copyright © 1943 by WILLIAMSON MUSIC
Copyright Renewed
International Copyright Secured   All Rights Reserved

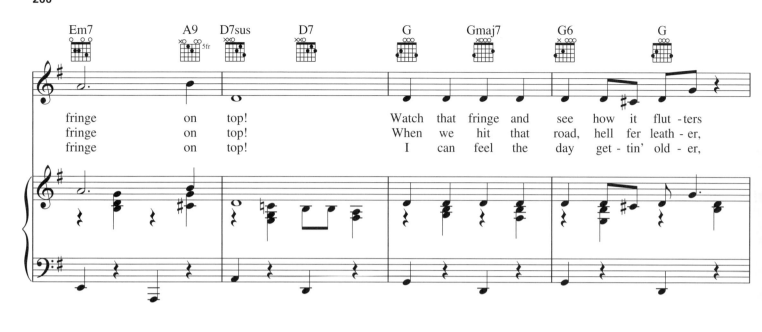

fringe   on   top!   Watch   that   fringe   and   see   how   it   flut - ters
fringe   on   top!   When   we   hit   that   road,   hell   fer   leath - er,
fringe   on   top!   I   can   feel   the   day   get - tin'   old - er,

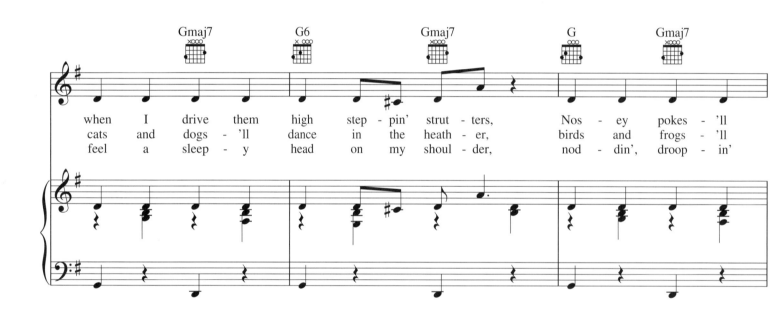

when   I   drive   them   high   step - pin'   strut - ters,   Nos - ey   pokes - 'll
cats   and   dogs - 'll   high   dance   in   the   heath - er,   birds   and   frogs - 'll
feel   a   sleep - y   head   on   my   shoul - der,   nod - din',   droop - in'

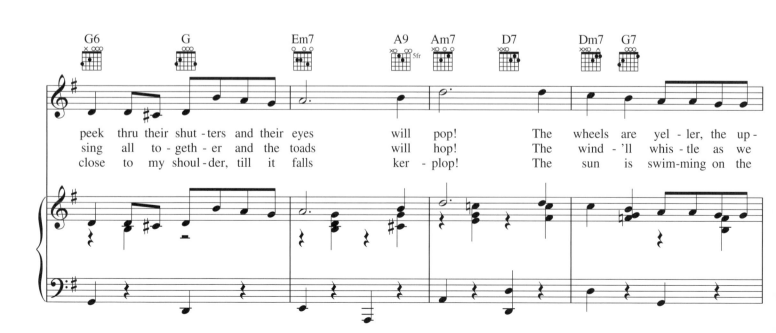

peek   thru   their   shut - ters   and   their   eyes   will   pop!   The   wheels   are   yel - ler,   the   up -
sing   all   to - geth - er   and   the   toads   will   hop!   The   wind - 'll   whis - tle   as   we
close   to   my   shoul - der,   till   it   falls   ker - plop!   The   sun   is   swim - ming   on   the

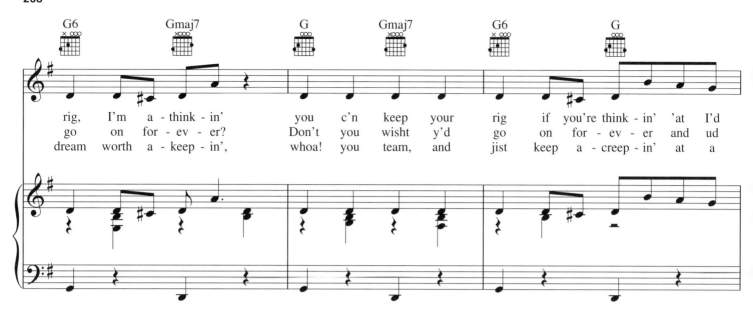

rig, I'm a-think-in' you c'n keep your rig if you're think-in' 'at I'd
go on for-ev-er? Don't you wisht y'd go on for-ev-er and ud
dream worth a-keep-in', whoa! you team, and jist keep a-creep-in' at a

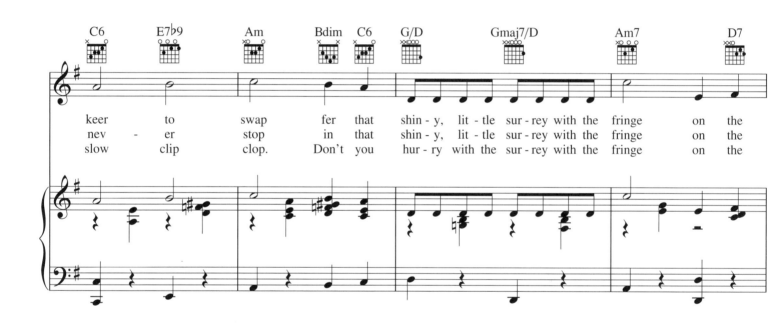

keer to swap fer that shin-y, lit-tle sur-rey with the fringe on the
nev - er stop in that shin-y, lit-tle sur-rey with the fringe on the
slow clip clop. Don't you hur-ry with the sur-rey with the fringe on the

top!
top!   top! _____

THAT OLD BLACK MAGIC

from the Paramount Picture STAR SPANGLED RHYTHM

Words by JOHNNY MERCER
Music by HAROLD ARLEN

old black mag - ic has me in its spell. That
old black mag - ic that you weave so well. Those
i - cy fin - gers up and down my spine. The

Copyright © 1942 Sony/ATV Music Publishing LLC
Copyright Renewed
All Rights Administered by Sony/ATV Music Publishing LLC, 8 Music Square West, Nashville, TN 37203
International Copyright Secured   All Rights Reserved

TANGERINE

from the Paramount Picture THE FLEET'S IN

Words by JOHNNY MERCER
Music by VICTOR SCHERTZINGER

Copyright © 1942 Sony/ATV Music Publishing LLC
Copyright Renewed
All Rights Administered by Sony/ATV Music Publishing LLC, 8 Music Square West, Nashville, TN 37203
International Copyright Secured   All Rights Reserved

A7
D7
Gm
Gm/F
3fr
3
tine.
Yes, she has them all on the
Em7
A7
Dm7
F/G
G7
3
run, but her heart be - longs to just one. Her
B♭
Gm7
Gm7/C
C7
1
F
Cm/E♭
3fr
heart be - longs to Tan - ger - ine.
D7
D7♯5
2
F
F6/9
Tan - ger - ine.
rit.

THANKS FOR THE MEMORY

from the Paramount Picture BIG BROADCAST OF 1938

Words and Music by LEO ROBIN
and RALPH RAINGER

Thanks for the mem-o-ry of
Thanks for the mem-o-ry of

can-dle-light and wine, ___ cas-tles on the Rhine, ___ the
sen-ti-men-tal verse, ___ noth-ing in my purse, ___ and

Par-the-non and mo-ments on the Hud-son Riv-er Line. ___ How
chuck-les when the preach-er said, "For bet-ter or for worse." ___ How

Copyright © 1937 Sony/ATV Music Publishing LLC
Copyright Renewed
All Rights Administered by Sony/ATV Music Publishing LLC, 8 Music Square West, Nashville, TN 37203
International Copyright Secured   All Rights Reserved

THAT'S AMORÉ
(That's Love)
from the Paramount Picture THE CADDY

Words by JACK BROOKS
Music by HARRY WARREN

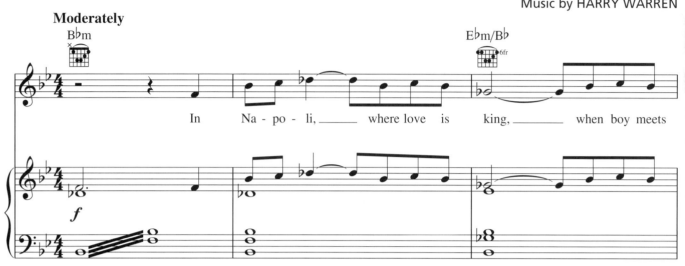

Copyright © 1953 Sony/ATV Music Publishing LLC and Four Jays Music
Copyright Renewed
All Rights on behalf of Sony/ATV Music Publishing LLC Administered by Sony/ATV Music Publishing LLC, 8 Music Square West, Nashville, TN 37203
International Copyright Secured   All Rights Reserved

THE VERY THOUGHT OF YOU

Words and Music by
RAY NOBLE

Copyright © 1934 Campbell Connelly Inc. and Warner Bros. Inc.
Copyright renewed; extended term of Copyright deriving from Ray Noble assigned and effective April 16, 1990 to Range Road Music Inc. and Bug Music-Quartet Music
This arrangement Copyright © 1993 Range Road Music Inc. and Bug Music-Quartet Music
International Copyright Secured   All Rights Reserved
Used by Permission

THAT'S LIFE

Words and Music by DEAN KAY
and KELLY GORDON

Copyright © 1964, 1966 UNIVERSAL - POLYGRAM INTERNATIONAL PUBLISHING, INC.
Copyright Renewed
All Rights Reserved   Used by Permission

294

TWO SLEEPY PEOPLE

from the Paramount Motion Picture THANKS FOR THE MEMORY

Words by FRANK LOESSER
Music by HOAGY CARMICHAEL

Copyright © 1938 Sony/ATV Music Publishing LLC
Copyright Renewed
All Rights Administered by Sony/ATV Music Publishing LLC, 8 Music Square West, Nashville, TN 37203
International Copyright Secured All Rights Reserved

The Way You Look Tonight

from SWING TIME

Words by DOROTHY FIELDS
Music by JEROME KERN

Copyright © 1936 UNIVERSAL - POLYGRAM INTERNATIONAL PUBLISHING, INC. and ALDI MUSIC
Copyright Renewed
Print Rights for ALDI MUSIC in the U.S. Controlled and Administered by HAPPY ASPEN MUSIC LLC c/o SHAPIRO, BERNSTEIN & CO., INC.
All Rights Reserved   Used by Permission

WHAT NOW MY LOVE
(Original French Title: "Et Maintenant")

Original French Lyric by PIERRE DELANOE
Music by GILBERT BECAUD
English Adaptation by CARL SIGMAN

Moderate Bolero tempo

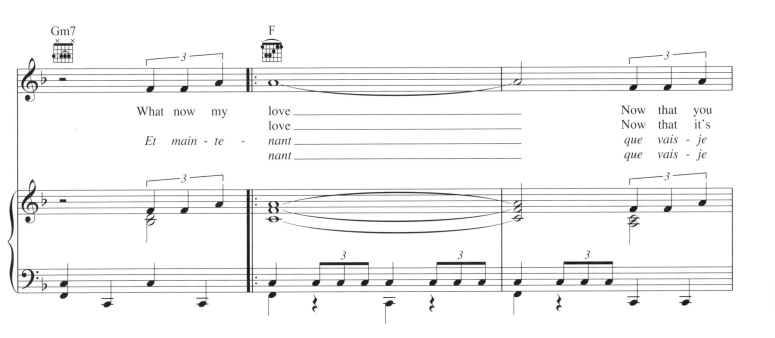

What now my love ___
love ___
Et main-te-nant ___
nant ___

Now that you
Now that it's
que vais-je
que vais-je

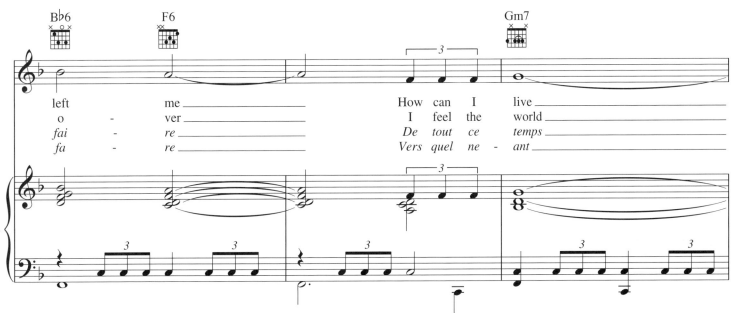

left me ___
o-ver ___
fai-re ___
fa-re ___

How can I live ___
I feel the world ___
De tout ce temps ___
Vers quel ne-ant ___

Copyright © 1961 by Editions Rideau Rouge, BMG Music Publishing France and Major Songs
Copyright Renewed
All Rights for Editions Rideau Rouge and BMG Music Publishing France Administered in the U.S. by BMG Songs, a division of BMG Music Publishing NA, Inc.
All Rights for Major Songs Administered by Bug Music
International Copyright Secured   All Rights Reserved

WITCHCRAFT

Music by CY COLEMAN
Lyrics by CAROLYN LEIGH

Shades of old Lu- cre- tia Bor- gia! There's a dev- il in you to- night,__ 'n' al- though my heart a- dores __ ya, my head says __ it ain't right, __ right to let you

© 1957 MORLEY MUSIC CO.
Copyright Renewed and Assigned to MORLEY MUSIC CO. and NOTABLE MUSIC COMPANY, INC.
All Rights for NOTABLE MUSIC COMPANY, INC. Administered by CHRYSALIS MUSIC
All Rights Reserved   Used by Permission

YOU BROUGHT A NEW KIND OF LOVE TO ME

from the Paramount Picture THE BIG POND

Words and Music by SAMMY FAIN,
IRVING KAHAL and PIERRE NORMAN

Copyright © 1930 Sony/ATV Music Publishing LLC
Copyright Renewed
All Rights Administered by Sony/ATV Music Publishing LLC, 8 Music Square West, Nashville, TN 37203
International Copyright Secured   All Rights Reserved

WIVES AND LOVERS
(Hey, Little Girl)
from the Paramount Picture WIVES AND LOVERS

Words by HAL DAVID
Music by BURT BACHARACH

Copyright © 1963 Sony/ATV Music Publishing LLC
Copyright Renewed
All Rights Administered by Sony/ATV Music Publishing LLC, 8 Music Square West, Nashville, TN 37203
International Copyright Secured All Rights Reserved

YESTERDAYS

from ROBERTA

Words by OTTO HARBACH
Music by JEROME KERN

Copyright © 1933 UNIVERSAL - POLYGRAM INTERNATIONAL PUBLISHING, INC.
Copyright Renewed
All Rights Reserved   Used by Permission

YOU DON'T KNOW WHAT LOVE IS

Words and Music by DON RAYE
and GENE DePAUL

Copyright © 1941 UNIVERSAL MUSIC CORP.
Copyright Renewed
All Rights Reserved   Used by Permission